TRACK
CHRISTIAN
LIFE

A STUDENT'S GUIDE TO
GRIEF

CHRISTIAN
FOCUS

tym

Copyright © Paul Tautges 2024

paperback ISBN 978-1-5271-1177-6

ebook ISBN 978-1-5271-1207-0

10 9 8 7 6 5 4 3 2 1

First published in 2024

by

Christian Focus Publications Ltd,

Geanies House, Fearn,

Ross-shire, IV20 1TW, Great Britain

www.christianfocus.com

with

Reformed Youth Ministries,

1445 Rio Road East Suite 201D

Charlottesville, Virginia, 22911

Cover by MOOSE77

Printed and bound by Gutenberg, Malta

CONTENTS

Series Introduction

Christianity is a religion of words, because our God is a God of words. He created through words, calls Himself the Living Word, and wrote a book (filled with words) to communicate to His children. In light of this, pastors and parents should take great efforts to train the next generation to be readers. *Track* is a series designed to do exactly that.

Written for students, the *Track* series addresses a host of topics in three primary areas: Doctrine, Culture, and the Christian Life. *Track's* booklets are theologically rich, yet accessible. They seek to engage and challenge the student without dumbing things down.

One definition of a track reads: *a way that has been formed by someone else's footsteps.* The goal of the *Track* series is to point us to that 'someone else'—Jesus Christ. The One who forged a track to guide His followers. While we cannot follow this track perfectly, by His grace and Spirit He calls us to strive to stay on the path. It is our prayer that this series of books would help guide Christ's Church until He returns.

In His service,

John Perritt
RYM's Director of Resources
Series Editor

1. Loss is Everywhere

Loss comes in many forms: a car accident that takes the life of a close friend, divorce in the family, college disappointments, friendships that dissolve because of conflict or long-distance moves, tragic school shootings, broken engagements, or job losses—just to name a few. Whatever way loss delivers grief to the doorstep of our hearts; the God of all comfort stands ready to bring comfort. We are not the first to endure the unbearable pain we know of as grief. Therefore, we can find comfort in knowing how God cares for us in times of sorrow.

THE ORIGIN OF GRIEF

Before sin entered the Garden of Eden, all was well and good. There was no loss, pain, grief, or death. Sadly, this heaven-on-earth didn't last long. The great deceiver, the devil, entered human experience and tempted Adam and Eve to doubt the goodness of God and the integrity of His Word, and they fell into his trap (Gen. 3:1-7).

The first man and woman betrayed God and, as a result, peaceful fellowship with their Creator turned to animosity. Excessive work, conflict, death, and grief entered their world and ours—all because of sin. And not one of us is exempt from its reach, as Job 5:7 testifies, 'man is born for trouble as sparks fly upward.' Adam's sin spread to all men and, therefore, just as sure as sparks rise out of a campfire, so every one of us suffers loss. Therefore, we should not be 'surprised at the fiery ordeal' when it comes (1 Pet. 4:12). Grief is part of everyday existence, but God abounds in grace and kindness toward us.

Early on, God sacrificed an animal for Adam and Eve to make a covering for their sin. Then He promised to send one man, born of a woman, to redeem sinners and deal a death blow to the devil (Gen. 3:14-15). The Bible then traces the progress and fulfillment of this promise throughout its pages. In God's perfect timing and manner, He sent this man—His one and only Son—into the world to live a sinless life and die a sinner's death in our place (Heb. 2:14-15). Jesus never sinned, but He died the death that every sinner deserves and rose from the grave on the third day. As a result, all who now turn to Him in humble, repentant faith receive the gracious gift of righteousness (Rom. 5:17; 2 Cor. 5:21). One day in the future, Jesus, the king of Kings will return to right all wrongs and put an end to our suffering by escorting us into God's eternal presence. Until then, the Word of God assures us of His faithful comfort.

THERE IS COMFORT IN CHRIST

The gospel portion of the Old Testament book of Isaiah begins with these words: '"Comfort, O comfort My people," says your God' (Isa. 40:1). Over the course of church history, Isaiah earned the nickname 'the evangelical prophet' because of his emphasis on the good news of the coming Messiah—the hope and strong comfort of Israel. Regarding this verse, Warren Wiersbe explains, 'The English word "comfort" comes from two Latin words that together mean "with strength."' When Isaiah says, "Be comforted!" it is not a word of pity but of power. God's comfort does not weaken us; it strengthens us. God is not indulging us but empowering us.'[1]

---

1   Warren W. Wiersbe, *Be Comforted* (Wheaton, IL: Scripture Press, 1992), 7.

Isaiah grounds this hope in God's relationship to Israel as His people: '"Comfort *My* people," says *your* God.' (Emphasis added). Even though His people's sin was worthy of a double portion of divine discipline, God would never turn His back on them. Instead, He would fulfill the covenant that He made with them. Later, through the mouth of Jeremiah, God again dispensed hope during Israel's pain: '"For I know the plans that I have for you," declares the Lord, "plans for welfare and not for calamity to give you a future and a hope"' (Jer. 29:11). Both prophets provided Messiah-centered comfort to their hearers by turning their focus away from their past, and from their present, toward the future hope of the promised kingdom.

Since we live *after* the cross of Calvary, we may refer to this as *Christ-centered comfort*, but the nature of the comfort God offers to us is much the same. God's comfort comes from His promise to those who believe in Christ, that the glory He will one day share with us far outweighs our present suffering (Phil. 1:6; Rom. 8:18).

The gospel offers Christ-centered hope that enables us to face the reality of death head-on. It holds forth the gift of eternal life which Jesus purchased with His own blood. Joni Eareckson Tada and Steve Estes write in their book *When God Weeps*:

> Earth's pain keeps crushing our hopes, reminding us this world can never satisfy; only heaven can. And every time we begin to nestle too comfortably on this planet, God cracks open the locks of the dam to allow an ice-cold splash of suffering to wake us from our spiritual slumber.[2]

Therefore, we must not waste these precious and painful occasions, which open the door to receiving God's mercy and seeing the fruit of the gospel in our hearts and the hearts of others.

THE GOAL OF THIS BOOK

My aim is to point you to the only lasting comfort—the comfort that is rooted in the gospel and the relational work of the one God who exists in three persons. God the Father pays attention to you in the wake of whatever causes your pain, and He shows His love in the many ways He cares for you (Matt. 6:32). Jesus Christ is the gentle and humble Son of God (Matt. 11:29), who turns His compassionate

---

2   Joni Eareckson Tada and Steve Estes, *When God Weeps* (Grand Rapids, MI: Zondervan, 1997), 202.

heart toward you (Matt. 9:36). He is the suffering Savior who experienced unimaginable grief throughout His life and, ultimately, during the last days leading up to His sacrificial death on your behalf (Isa. 53:3-12). The Father and the Son commissioned and sent the Holy Spirit to be your comforter, who applies the healing words of Scripture to your aching heart (John 14:16).

A tender scene from J. R. R. Tolkien's *The Return of the King* provides a fitting conclusion to this chapter and a transition to the rest of this book. To comfort and instruct Pippin, whose mind was being overtaken by fear of losing his best friend, Aragorn the king says, "His grief he will not forget; but it will not darken his heart, it will teach him wisdom."[3] Some losses change us forever; we never forget them for as long as we live. Yet grief can be our teacher if we look to our hope in Christ, and humbly let it do its God-appointed work in us.

MAIN POINT

Grief is part of living in our broken world, but God's comfort is readily available to us through Jesus.

---

3   J. R. R. Tolkien, *The Return of the King* (New York: Houghton Mifflin Company, 1955, ren. 1983), 145.

QUESTIONS FOR REFLECTION

- What kinds of losses have you experienced in your life? Which has been the most difficult for you to accept?
- What does it mean to think of comfort being rooted in the gospel?
- How might seeing comfort this way help you grow in your relationship with the Lord?

2. Shock and Tears

'Grandpa died,' my mom said when her phone call from Grandma ended. I was a sophomore in high school.

After retiring from his career as an assembler of wood-paneled station wagons at the Ford Motor Company, my mom's father spent every morning working in his garden. One day in May, after returning to the house and eating a small lunch, he lay down for a nap. An hour later, Grandma couldn't wake him. Her husband of fifty-nine years had suffered a massive heart attack. The news hit me hard.

Since my father's dad died when I was only three years old, I have no memory of him. But my mom's dad made priceless memories throughout my childhood. Every summer, he took my brothers and me fishing on Cowboy Lake and taught us how to scale, fillet, and fry our catch. Losing Grandpa pained my siblings and me. Still, this didn't fully prepare us for the following spring.

One year later, a young man murdered my favorite uncle. I still remember where I was standing when my mom told me how Dad and the police found his body. By *favorite*, I mean Uncle Denny was the uncle we were closest to. We loved all our aunts and uncles, but we had a closer connection with him for two reasons. First, he lived only fifteen minutes from our house, so we saw him more often. Second, his wife died in a motorcycle accident after only one year of marriage, so Uncle Denny found affection and a break from loneliness by coming to our house on major holidays. Every Christmas, for example, he would join us for dinner. Later, after he went home, Mom would pass out the envelopes he had slipped to her privately, each containing a crisp $20 bill. Believe me, to a kid in the 1970s, that was big money! Losing our uncle was painful, but the manner of his death heightened our loss.

No matter how death enters our lives, it's hard to lose those we love. There is often shock and tears. But there is also comfort available from God.

COMFORT FROM THE TRIUNE GOD

Several years after the deaths of my grandfather and uncle, I came to know Jesus through a home Bible study in the Gospel of John. Since I grew up in a religion that taught salvation by good works and religious rituals, I didn't understand how God freely offered salvation to me through the finished work of Jesus. I'm forever grateful to the Lord for opening my eyes to my need to repent, to turn from my sin and faith in my good works and turn to Christ in humble faith to receive the gracious gift of God (Eph. 2:8-9). Later, by sitting under biblical teaching and experiencing God's grace mediated through His people, I began confidently tapping into the comfort of God in Christ. Therefore, I want to come alongside you in your time of suffering to convey key biblical truths that I have learned, which will bring you comfort and eternal perspective.

The Bible tells us that God is Trinitarian: Father, Son, and Holy Spirit, and all three persons of the godhead go to work for His children when you suffer. Therefore, when grief overshadows your soul, you can run to God for help and comfort. As mentioned in the last chapter, the heavenly Father knows all your needs and is aware of every loss you go through in this broken world (Matt. 6:8, 32). Also, the Son of God is your compassionate High Priest who understands human weakness and prays for you at the right hand of God (Heb. 4:14-16; 7:25). And, in Christ, the Holy Spirit becomes your helper who unites you to Jesus by faith and prays for you, especially when the hurt and confusion are so raw that you don't know what to say (Rom. 8:26-27). Yet, God has provided an even more tangible means of comfort—His people. Fellow Christians may serve as God-with-skin-on, in the sense that they administer His grace to us in tangible ways.

COMFORT FROM THE FAMILY OF GOD

God never intended for any of us to go through life's challenges alone. As the Father, Son, and Spirit have enjoyed perfect fellowship from eternity, so they created us in their image and for relationship.

Before they rebelled, Adam and Eve walked with God in perfect harmony, but sin disrupted that peaceful relationship. So, the Creator implemented His plan to resolve the root problem humanity caused. The Creator became the Redeemer, and God became man in the person of Jesus Christ. Through faith, Jesus reconciles us to God (Col. 1:22). This means He alone bridges the infinite chasm between us and God—a chasm created by our sin—and He brings us back to God (1 Pet. 3:18). But the Spirit also immerses us in the body of Christ; He secures for us a relationship with all believers everywhere (1 Cor. 12:13). God adopts us into His family (Eph. 1:5).

What does all this mean? It means we need each other. It means you don't have to go it alone. Why? God created you for relationship. First, He designed you for a relationship with Himself. Second, when you know the Lord through faith in Jesus, you become part of a spiritual family whose members are called to comfort one another (2 Cor 1:3-5). This comfort finds its simplest and most beautiful expression in the familial relationships in the local church. In the family of God, you can experience soul satisfying comfort from brothers and sisters committed to doing life with you.

COMFORT FROM THE WORD OF GOD

One of the chief means by which the Spirit comforts your heart is the truth of Scripture. For example, the psalmist testifies, 'He sent His word and healed them' (Ps.107:20). Since the Holy Spirit is the member of the Trinity who breathed out the thoughts of God to men, who then recorded them in Scripture (2 Tim. 3:16; 2 Pet. 1:21; 1 Cor. 2:11-13), He employs these same words to apply healing truth to your broken heart. The Spirit illumines your mind and shines light on the promises of God and their application to your various trials.

Jesus assures us of this confidence as well. Shortly after He informs the disciples that He will leave them, they express much grief. In response, Jesus promises to send another helper, the Spirit of truth, who will remind them of what He taught and bring peace to their hearts (John 16:12-14). As a follower of Jesus, the Spirit's never-ending presence strengthens you and delivers the comfort of God's healing words. Scripture is a medicinal balm to the pain of grief and will strengthen your trust in God.

Regardless of the various depths of pain and the kinds of loss you may endure in this life, God will meet you in your grief. Through Scripture and His people, God will comfort your heart and nurture your faith.

MAIN POINT

Loss is often unexpected, but comfort comes to you through the Father, Son, and Spirit as you pray, read Scripture, and fellowship with the people of God.

QUESTIONS FOR REFLECTION

- What emotions did you experience when you first received news of a significant loss? If considerable time has passed since then, how are your emotions different now?
- What ways have people helped you work through your grief?
- Are there any Scriptures that have been especially comforting?

3. Hide in God, not from God

When the dark shadow of grief creeps in and threatens your inner peace, it may tempt you to hide—to be alone. You might want time to think or cry in private, which is not always bad. However, escape becomes unhealthy when it becomes a pattern. Like our first parents, we are prone to hide not only from others but from the only One who can ultimately help us and heal our deepest wounds.

Yes, Adam and Eve hid from God because they were guilty of disobeying His command to not eat from a certain tree in the garden. However, they also hid from God because they felt exposed. For the first time, they realized they were naked—fully seen (compare Gen. 2:25 with Gen. 3:7). Grief has a curious way of doing that to us, especially when our loss is public.

Suicide, for example, is a loss that leaves friends and family feeling even more exposed than a natural death. It opens them up to having tough conversations when news of the way their loved one died becomes known. False guilt and shame often plague those who remain. Pastor and police chaplain, Bruce Ray, shares this insight in *Help! Someone I Love Died by Suicide*:

> Suicide adds complications to the grieving process, such as gnawing questions that beg for answers, misdirected anger, a need to assign blame for what happened, false guilt for not seeing the signs or doing something to prevent the suicide, or shame that someone you love took his or her own life. Grieving suicide will likely be a long and difficult work … Grieving a suicide also often involves shame. There is a disgrace associated with suicide that is not found with other deaths.[1]

Just as an injured animal runs to a hideout to lick its wounds, the pain of shame can tempt you to run from God. But God's arms are always open when you feel hurt or damaged. Therefore, you should not hide *from* God, but hide *in* God.

---

1   Bruce Ray, *Help! Someone I Love Died by Suicide* (Wapwallopen, PA: Shepherd Press, 2019), 35.

GOD IS YOUR HIDING PLACE AND STRENGTH

Instead of *running from God* when your pain is acute, you need to *run to Him*, since He is your 'refuge and strength, a very present help in trouble' (Ps. 46:1). Therefore, God is the One you can talk to about what hurts right now and what makes you fearful about the future. When loss takes the wind out of your sails, God will be your source of strength.

> *Do you not know? Have you not heard?*
> *The Everlasting God, the Lord, the Creator of*
> *the ends of the earth*
> *Does not become tired or grow weary.*
> *There is no searching of His understanding.*
> *He gives strength to the weary,*
> *And to him who has no might*
> *He increases power.*
> *Though youths grow weary and tired,*
> *And vigorous young men stumble badly,*
> *But those who wait for the Lord*
> *Will gain new strength; and renew*
> *their power;*
> *They will lift up their wings like eagles,*
> *They will run and not become weary,*
> *They will walk and not grow tired.*
>
> (Isa. 40:28-31)

The sovereign Lord never gets weak or wiped out, as you and I do. He's always ready to work on your behalf, even while you sleep (Ps. 127:2). And there is nowhere you may go that the Holy Spirit will not be there with you (Ps. 139:7). God is your very present help. 'The eternal God is a dwelling place, and underneath are the everlasting arms' (Deut. 33:27).

If Jesus is your Lord and Savior, then you are never alone. God invites you into His unfailing presence. The Holy Spirit seals you in Christ and gives you a promise. The Lord Himself 'has said, "I will never desert you, nor will I ever forsake you"' (Heb. 13:5). God is your refuge, strength, and ever-present help. He is your hiding place.

GOD NOTICES YOUR TEARS

Your grief is important to God. It must be, considering the personal testimony revealed in King David's song lyrics: 'You have taken account of my wanderings; put my tears in Your bottle. Are they not in Your book?' (Ps. 56:8). God tracks your life, including all the people and events that bring you sorrow. He grieves for the brokenness caused by sin, which changed His perfect world into one filled with evil, pain, and loss (Gen. 6:5-6). And since

God created you in His image, you are free to grieve.

In Psalm 56, David pleads with God to give him strength, and reminds himself of the promises of God: 'This I know, that God is for me' (Ps. 56:9). Interestingly, the Apostle Paul encourages us with essentially the same promise but connects it to Christ.

> *What then shall we say to these things? If God is for us, who is against us? He who did not spare His own Son, but delivered Him over for us all, how will He not also with Him freely give us all things?* (Rom. 8:31-32)

If God did not hold back His one and only Son but gave Him up to be the redeeming sacrifice for your sins, then there is no other need you have now that He will not meet.

When you grieve, it might feel as if God is against you. But your feelings are not the ultimate authority; the Word of God is the only sure anchor for your soul. Therefore, when you know Jesus as your Savior and Lord, you can speak biblical truth to yourself. While you allow your God-given emotions freedom to work, you must also employ the promises of God to keep your emotions from controlling you.

So, cry your heart out. God will not mind. He will listen and speak the words of peace you need. He will steady your heart with His promises.

GOD DRAWS NEAR TO YOU

Many biblical promises help you, but perhaps the most valuable of all when grief overwhelms you is this: *God is near*. The reason for this is that grief may cause you to feel shades of abandonment, which result in loneliness. Even in a crowded room, you and I can feel completely alone. Therefore, one anchoring promise is Psalm 34:18, 'The Lord is near to the brokenhearted and saves those who are crushed in spirit.'

In his devotional commentary, *Psalms by the Day*, Alec Motyer tells us that the Hebrew word for near refers to a person's next of kin, who takes on himself the needs of another family member.[2] What a tender word picture this is! The perfect work of our Savior, the Lord Jesus Christ, secures God's presence for you. The Son of God became Immanuel, God with us, our 'next of kin' who wants to carry our burdens with us. In Christ, God has drawn near

---

2   Alec Motyer, *Psalms by the Day* (Fearn, Scotland: Christian Focus, 2016), 87.

to us. Therefore, we can now draw near to God, especially when we need grace for our time of need (Heb. 4:15). God is close by. This is a rock-solid promise to cling to, especially when your emotions are all over the place.

Tim Challies, in his personal journaling following the sudden death of his twenty-year-old son, Nick, explains how clinging to the promise of the Lord's presence stabilizes the emotions: 'My feelings rotate like the earth; my emotions come and go like the seasons. But the truth is as fixed and constant as the sun. When I focus on what is true, I understand that God is present with me.'[3] In the Word of God, you have the fixed anchors you need on stormy days. His truth is 'as fixed and constant as the sun.' As sure as you can count on the sun to rise tomorrow morning, God will keep His promises.

God is your hiding place. Nothing can ever separate you from Him or His love (Rom. 8:39). He knows all about your sorrows and He comforts you with promises of His loving care and presence. His tender mercies are new every morning, and He draws near to you in your times of grief and loss.

---

3   Tim Challies, *Seasons of Sorrow* (Grand Rapids, MI: Zondervan Reflective, 2022), 51.

MAIN POINT

Grief exposes you to dangers of uncertainty and tempts you to turn away from God when you need Him most, but resting in the promise of His presence stabilizes your soul.

QUESTIONS FOR REFLECTION

- In times of grief, are you tempted to hide? If so, what baby step can you take to move toward God and others, rather than away from them?
- Besides Psalms 46:1 and 34:18, what other Bible promises comfort you? If you can't think of any, look at the list of recommended Scriptures at the end of this book.

4. Adjust Your Focus

When I was fifteen years old, I made my first big purchase. For months, I saved wages from my dishwashing job at a local restaurant. When the big day came, my older brother drove me to a large electronics store where I bought my first 35mm camera, an extra-long zoom lens, foldable tripod, and a fancy green canvas bag to carry my new gadgets. In the remaining years of high school, I spent countless hours experimenting with the art of photography. Though none of my photos ever became magazine worthy, I received joy from learning the art of focusing on the right object while the background faded from view.

In a similar way, learning to look through biblical lenses and correct our focus is essential in times of grief and loss. Walking through the fog of loss requires fine tuning our heart's focus to God-centered truths that speak stability to our souls and help background clutter to fade.

LOOK TO GOD'S COVENANT-KEEPING FAITHFULNESS

The Bible refers to death as our last *enemy* (1 Cor. 15:26). This explains, in part, why the death of someone close to you can feel like a personal attack—as if part of you died with them. It can feel like the enemy of death ripped your heart out of your chest and left you bleeding on the floor. Abraham felt this way when his wife Sarah died. Yet he remembered the covenant-keeping faithfulness of God.

Throughout their sixty-plus years of marriage, Abraham and Sarah had been through a lot; their hearts were bound to the other's just as God originally planned for the one-flesh relationship of marriage (Gen. 2:24). But Sarah's death severed their bond and Abraham mourned and wept for her. Later, he purchased a cave to honor Sarah by giving her a proper burial (Gen. 23:9). By purchasing this cemetery plot in the land of Canaan, Abraham turned his heart to focus on God's faithfulness and trusted Him to keep His promise: 'To your descendants I have given this land' (Gen. 15:18). Many years later, one of Abraham's descendants would follow in his footsteps.

Betrayed as a teenager, Abraham's great-grandson, Joseph, endured much suffering which comprised various kinds of loss, including betrayal, being fired from his job, and being imprisoned because of the false accusation of sexual assault (Gen. 39:11-20). Yet, near the end of his life, Joseph instructed his formerly estranged brothers to remember to bring his bones with them when they left Egypt to enter the land of promise (Gen. 50:25).

Both Abraham and Joseph displayed the forward look of faith. Despite pain and loss, they looked to the God who had made a covenant with His people. They tied their faith to the promise of God's inheritance and anchored their broken hearts to His faithfulness. You can do the same.

LOOK TO GOD'S COMPASSION

During their time in the wilderness, God's people depended on Him to supply their daily bread, heavenly bread, literally. Every morning, they awoke to find sweet, flaky bread on the ground. Never had they seen such a thing, so they called it *manna*, meaning *what is it?* (Exod. 16:13-21). Moses told them to gather it up quickly because the sun would melt it away. God designed their morning habit of gathering just enough for that day to train them to trust Him to provide until the next day, when a fresh supply would appear. God's compassions are like that, says Jeremiah.

The Lord's lovingkindnesses indeed never cease, for His compassions never fail. They are new every morning; great is Your faithfulness. (Lam. 3:22-23)

Like healthy leftovers in your refrigerator, yesterday's promises provide some nourishment. But for your relationship with the Lord to thrive, your soul needs a conscious awareness of fresh mercies from God, which He provides every morning. You will receive strength from these new mercies as you feed your soul on His Word. It was this way for Jeremiah when he grieved the loss of God's city.

Lamenting over the destruction of God's city, the prophet begins by humbly bringing his despair to God in prayer. Then he deliberately remembers the unchanging character of God. This leads to spiritual refreshment and renewed worship, for the 'Lord's lovingkindnesses indeed never cease.' In the preceding verse, he calls to mind the mercies of the Lord, which become the reason he can say, 'I have hope' (v. 21). Like Jeremiah, when the pain of loss blurs your spiritual vision, you can look to the Lord. The Lord's compassion and mercy do not fail. They are new every morning.

The word 'lovingkindnesses' is related to the Hebrew word for *womb* and communicates tender care and affection. Yahweh's grace and tender care never end. They never fail, never cease; they are 'new every morning.' Just as God's people found manna on the ground every morning for forty years in the wilderness, as a daily expression of God's loyal love (Exod. 16:35; Neh. 9:20-21), so you wake up to fresh mercies which are sufficient for today. Therefore, you can also praise Him for His faithfulness.

LOOK TO GOD'S PROMISE OF GLORY

Our souls currently inhabit bodies which are temporary; they will not live forever in their present form. Our bodies are an earthly means through which God magnifies His glory by accomplishing His purposes on earth, but one day every one of us will die. Yet God will one day resurrect these same bodies, and rejoin them to our spirits, to spend everlasting life in the new heavens and on the new earth.

Believers in Jesus Christ can be confident 'that if the tent which is our earthly home is destroyed, we have a building from God, a house not made with hands, eternal in the heavens' (2 Cor. 5:1 NKJV). Our 'flesh and blood cannot inherit the kingdom of God, nor does the perishable inherit the imperishable' (1 Cor. 15:50), but one day all who know Christ will receive a new, glorified body that will live forever with the Savior. When that glorious day comes, our perishable body will put on the imperishable, and our mortal body will put on immortality (15:53). This new, resurrected body will be the permanent house for our soul, and heaven will be our forever home. Even now, as you read this book, Jesus is preparing a place for those who trust in Him for their eternal salvation.

Before leaving earth and ascending to heaven, Jesus spoke these reassuring words to His followers:

"Do not let your heart be troubled; believe in God, believe also in Me. In My Father's house are many dwelling places; if it were not so, I would have told you; for I go to prepare

a place for you. If I go and prepare a place for you, I will come again and receive you to Myself, that where I am, there you may be also. And you know the way where I am going." Thomas said to Him, "Lord, we do not know where You are going, how do we know the way?" Jesus said to him, "I am the way, and the truth, and the life; no one comes to the Father but through Me. If you had known Me, you would have known My Father also; from now on you know Him, and have seen Him." (John 14:1-7)

Consider the simple promises found in these verses. God has a big house with many rooms, which surpasses anything you or I can imagine. Best of all, though, is that God will be there with us. Because of His presence, there will be no darkness there. Revelation 21:23 describes the heavenly city this way: 'the city has no need of the sun or of the moon to shine on it, for the glory of God has illumined it, and its lamp is the Lamb.'

One day, Jesus will return to bring all who belong to Him home. Perhaps the most wonderful assurance of all is that we can know the way to get there. Jesus is the way. He is the only way to the Father. As you grieve, remember these comforting promises for those who belong to Jesus.

MAIN POINT

To journey through the fog of grief, you need to learn to focus on God's faithful character and eternal promises.

QUESTIONS FOR REFLECTION

- What are one or two ways that grief naturally turns your focus away from God and to yourself?
- Read 1 Peter 1:3-5. God promises an everlasting inheritance to all those who are in Christ. How might meditating on this promise help you in times of grief?

5. Safety in the Storm

When I was a teenager, my dad and I witnessed the forming of a tornado cloud over a farm a few miles to the west of where I grew up. We only had enough time to tell Mom and my siblings to head to the basement for shelter. In a matter of moments, the black twister passed over our house, and all was eerily quiet. If we had not seen the cyclone forming while we were working in the yard, there would have been no advance notice and, therefore, no way of escape.

Nowadays, we have phone apps that notify us if a severe storm is on the way. Having this information can give us a taste of what it feels like to know the future, and this foreknowledge provides us with a bit of comfort, doesn't it? It helps us to avoid some dangers, prepare for the worst, and perhaps ease some anxiety by giving us a sense of control.

In a similar way, we sometimes wish God would give us advance notice before grief swirls our way. But God rarely does that. If He did, we might try harder to control our lives to avoid pain instead of learning to trust His goodness and grace. Deborah Howard, a hospice caregiver, exhorts us to believe beforehand that God is good and in control:

> We must have the essential faith and trust in God *before* our hearts are broken. Then we will possess the tools needed to understand and deal with the situation *without being devastated.*[1]

Dynamic faith in the Lord prepares us to face life's dangers.

GOD IS A VERY-PRESENT HELP

Psalm 46 offers a fountain of comfort and peace, along with a helpful application. The writer does not preoccupy himself with predicting when and where storms may come but with knowing the God who is the source of soul-rest during the storms.

---

1   Deborah Howard, *Sunsets: Reflections for Life's Final Journey* (Wheaton, IL: Crossway, 2005), p. 35.

God is our refuge and strength, a very present help in trouble. Therefore we will not fear, though the earth should change and though the mountains slip into the heart of the sea. (Ps. 46:1-2)

Let's dissect the psalmist's testimony into three assurances. First, he tells us that God is our *refuge*. God is a shelter for us. Scripture provides other images of God's safekeeping. For example, Moses paints a picture of God's strong and loving care: 'The eternal God is a dwelling place, and underneath are the everlasting arms' (Deut. 33:27). Second, God offers His support and 'strength.' He puts His power into action for us. His strength works *for us* in our times of weakness. Third, God is our 'very present help' in threatening times. God doesn't respond to our cries from a distance. Rather, He draws near. His presence is personal and active when we run to Him. This leads the author of Psalm 46 to assure us that God will help us with our fears.

As your ever-present help, the Lord invites you to talk to Him about your pain and weakness because of Christ, the high priest, who can 'sympathize' with the weaknesses of every sinner who turns to Him (Heb. 4:15).

As a result, you can 'approach the throne of grace with confidence, so that you may receive mercy and find grace for help at the time of our need' (Heb. 4:16).

A THEOLOGY OF REFUGE WILL ANCHOR YOU TO HOPE

When the Lord is your refuge, you will have strength to face your fears—even the fear of your own death or the death of a loved one.

When a close loved one returns from a visit to the cancer specialist and tells you that nothing more can be done, that 'it is only a matter of time,' your heart and voice may immediately cry out in fear and grief. Your pain is real, but you do not have to give in to fear and despair. God is your refuge, especially in these times and, therefore, you need not fear. *Trusting God dispels all other fears because He is sovereign over life and death.* Death is not final. God is in control and has promised ultimate victory in Jesus.

Using the imagery of waves, James Bruce writes about the genuine pain of grief and the hope that comes when we have a strong anchor:

Real grief is not easily comforted. It comes like ocean waves rushing up the sand, subsiding back, only to roll in again. These waves vary in size, frequency, and intensity. Some are small, lapping up around the feet. Others are stronger; they foam the water around you and cause you to stagger. Then there are the overwhelming waves with an under-tow that can turn your world upside down and drag you out into deep waters. In times such as those, the mourner desperately needs an anchor.[2]

The anchor to hold onto is God. As you trust in Him, you remain unshakeable, safe, and secure in His tender care. No matter how difficult your storm may be, you can endure it with inner calm and joy. 'There is a river whose streams make glad the city of God, the holy dwelling places of the Most High' (Ps. 46:4).

Again, the Lord assures us of His presence: 'God is in the midst of her, she will not be moved; God will help her when morning dawns' (v. 5). It is peaceful in the city of God, where He dwells. Even when circumstances are beyond your control, you are exactly where He wants you to be. In your grief, learn to trust Him. He delights in coming to our aid.

---

2   James W. Bruce, III, *From Grief to Glory: A Book of Comfort for Grieving Parents* (Edinburgh: Banner of Truth, 2008), 70-71.

GOD'S COMFORTING PRESENCE IS AN ANTIDOTE TO ANXIETY

Psalm 46 counsels us to quiet ourselves. Inner peace doesn't simply happen while we remain passive. Our will must be engaged. God makes this clear when He says, '*Cease striving* and know that I am God' (Ps. 46:10). The Hebrew word translated *cease* means to sink or relax. And *striving* is a term that typically refers to warfare. God's admonition may be stated this way: 'Be at peace. Relax. I am God. You are not. I am the conqueror. I am Lord of all the earth. And I am all of this for your personal safety.' But the psalmist also reveals how we can plug into a real-time sense of God's safekeeping power. He counsels us, 'Come, behold the works of the Lord' (v. 8). When you feel your life is in an upheaval, you can experience God's peace by remembering His powerful deeds.

The way to be still, God says, is by knowing and trusting Him. It's by truly believing that He is who He says He is. He is the sovereign God who is in control. You and I are not. Your life is in His hands. Therefore, you can rest; you can relax your heart. The more you meditate on the works of the Lord, the more confident you become. God is saying, 'Stop worrying! I will have the victory. Stop acting as if this is your battle. Relax. Rest in me. Not only am I the God of the universe, but I am *your* God. I will be your peace.'

The psalm ends by repeating a key truth: 'The Lord of hosts is with us; the God of Jacob is our stronghold.' By stating the same truth three times, in slightly different ways, the psalmist is making a point: *During your storms, you can remember that God's presence is real.* He is not far away. He is very near in your grief and suffering.

MAIN POINT

When you feel threatened, you naturally seek ways of escape, but the Lord is your only fail-safe storm shelter.

QUESTIONS FOR REFLECTION

- What are your favorite hiding places when life hurts? How are they inferior to the Lord? Talk to the Lord about them and ask Him to help you learn to run to Him first. Consider memorizing Psalm 46:1.
- Meditate on Psalm 32:7. How might this verse influence the way you pray when you feel threatened?

6. The Heavenly Father Cares

When my children were toddlers, they would sometimes run to me sobbing after something painful happened. To listen and show I cared, I bent down to look into their eyes. God does the same, as the psalmist testifies: 'Because He has inclined His ear to me, therefore I shall call upon Him as long as I live' (Ps. 116:2). The word *inclined* means 'bent down.' God bends down, turns His head, and listens to your cries for help. You might think of prayer as your feeble attempt to *reach up to God*. However, when you pray, *God lowers Himself to listen* because He cares (theologians refer to this as God's condescension).

The first person of the Trinity—the Father who freely sent His one and only Son to die for your sins and mine—is aware of your needs. He listens to your cries and delights to give you what is good for you. Knowing and believing this truth is a great comfort in times of grief. In this chapter and the next two, I will help you think about the loving care of the triune God.

YOUR FATHER LISTENS TO YOU

According to his opening words, the man who penned Psalm 116 had a deep hope and confidence in God's love and concern for him: 'I love the LORD, because He hears my voice and my supplications' (Ps. 116:1). The author, probably King David, prayed because he knew God would listen. Divine condescension, God's voluntary lowering of Himself, motivated David to open his heart to God. His admission is simple, raw, and emotional. His honesty is naked: *I love God because He hears me. And because He hears me, I pray.*

God is not far away, but 'near to the brokenhearted and saves those who are crushed in spirit' (Ps. 34:18). He is like a father who 'has compassion on His children' (Ps. 103:13). This fatherly condescension of our God and King reinforced the psalmist's confidence in God as the One who listens. Therefore, he resolves to call on Him as long as he lived.

The New Testament is even more explicit and intimate in its presentation of God as your heavenly Father. Not only does He care enough to listen to your cries, but He also has infinite knowledge of your needs, and a heart that delights to give the best gifts to those whom He predestined for adoption through Jesus Christ (Eph. 1:5).

YOUR FATHER KNOWS YOUR NEEDS

When the disciples asked Jesus to teach them how to pray, He made this amazing statement: 'Your Father knows what you need before you ask Him' (Matt. 6:8). Jesus does not call the first person of the Trinity '*the* Father of heaven and earth,' though that is true. Instead, He stresses the relational aspect, saying to us, '*your* Father.' Every Christian has a relationship with God that unbelievers do not. Yes, God is the Father of all in the sense that He is the Creator 'from whom are all things' (1 Cor. 8:6), but He is Father—*relationally*—only to followers of Jesus. This relationship is based on grace alone through faith in Christ alone, but deepens as you talk to your heavenly Father.

Your Father 'knows what you need before you ask Him.' This raises an honest question: if your faithful Father already knows your needs and promises to meet them, why bother to pray? But what happens next in the gospel account answers the question. 'Pray, then, in this way:

"Our Father, who is in heaven"' (Matt. 6:9). Because He knows and cares, you should pray. This strengthens your relationship. Later in the same chapter, Jesus restates how God's intimate knowledge should relieve your anxiety: 'your heavenly Father knows that you need all these things' (Matt. 6:32). Your loving Father knows what you need before you ask. Therefore, ask Him. Verbalize your needs to Him.

YOUR FATHER DELIGHTS IN YOU

Not only is God the source of all that is good, but He delights in you. In Luke's account, Jesus follows this teaching on prayer with a helpful comparison: 'If you then, being evil, know how to give good gifts to your children, how much more will your heavenly Father give the Holy Spirit to those who ask Him?' (Luke 11:13). If we, as sinful human beings, enjoy giving gifts, how much more does an infinitely good God know how to give what is good to His children?

Sometimes, however, what is good for us does not feel good. For example, the Apostle Paul prayed three times for God to remove a painful 'thorn in the flesh' (2 Cor. 12:7). But God withheld the apostle's request from him because the Spirit had deeper heart work that the apostle needed. In the end, Paul understood that even God's withholding was good for him, as he experienced the supernatural strength of Christ more vividly in his weakness.

Honest prayer cultivates humility. It requires acknowledgement of your helplessness. You ask God for help because He invites you to ask. And you ask because 'Every good thing given and every perfect gift is from above, coming down from the Father of lights' (James 1:17). The light of God's holiness and glory shines with infinite intensity. Therefore, God will not tempt you to sin or ever lead you into evil. If you ask Him for a fish, He will not give you a snake (Luke 11:11).

MAIN POINT

The heavenly Father cares for you, knows your needs, and wants you to talk to Him about what makes you sad or anxious.

QUESTIONS FOR REFLECTION

- Would you describe your prayers to God as being raw or naked, free from flowery language used to impress Him or gain entrance into His presence?
- How should the image of God lowering Himself to attentively listen to your cries for help change the way you pray?

- When was the last time you consciously thought about God's delight in you, as one of His blood-bought children? Take a moment to thank Him for His loving care.

7. Jesus Wept

―――――――

When I was a brand-new Christian, my future wife and I were helpers in the children's ministry of our church. One song the kids loved to sing had a chorus that went something like this: 'I am happy, happy, happy all day.' It was a fun song which, of course, included hand and body motions. However, the longer I walk with the Lord, the more I dislike the song. It simply doesn't give an accurate depiction of the Christian life. Yes, there is joy in knowing Christ—to be sure—but life also hurts badly. When life hurts, *heart-wrenching pain commonly coaches us to see all sadness as badness.* After all, if I'm supposed to be happy, happy, happy all the time, then why am I so sad, sad, sad? What is wrong with me?!

However, the life experience of our fully human Savior teaches us differently. The shortest verse in the Bible testifies, 'Jesus wept' (John 11:35). If grief affected the sinless Son of God, and He was not ashamed to express it openly before others, then surely being sad is not always bad. Jesus' response to loss and hurt instructs us to consider the goodness of sadness.

JESUS IS NOT ASHAMED OF SADNESS

When Jesus lost His close friend, Lazarus, He cried actual tears. The Gospel of John describes it this way:

Therefore, when Mary came where Jesus was, she saw Him, and fell at His feet, saying to Him, "Lord, if You had been here, my brother would not have died." When Jesus therefore saw her weeping, and the Jews who came with her also weeping, He was deeply moved in spirit and was troubled, and said, "Where have you laid him?" They said to Him, "Lord, come and see." Jesus wept. So the Jews were saying, "See how He loved him!" (John 11:32-36)

When the Holy Spirit impregnated the virgin Mary, the child who was conceived was truly the eternal Son of God in human form. As a result, Jesus is the godman, the only person qualified to be the 'one mediator also between God and men' (1 Tim. 2:5). Because Jesus humbled Himself and took on humanity, He can sympathize with our every weakness and sorrow, and give us the grace we need in times of loss.

JESUS GOT ANGRY AT DEATH

It is not immediately obvious in John's account, but there is a mixture of grief and anger in Jesus' response to the death of His friend. Jesus was 'deeply moved in spirit and was troubled' (John 11:33). This phrase exposes His inner agitation. When Jesus observed Mary weeping with grief, He groaned in His spirit and became angry. In his classic essay, *The Emotional Life of Our Lord,* first published in 1912, theologian B. B. Warfield writes:

> What John tells us, in point of fact, is that Jesus approached the grave of Lazarus, in a state, not of uncontrollable grief, but of irrepressible anger. He did respond … with quiet, sympathetic tears: "Jesus wept" (verse 36). But the emotion which tore his breast and clamored for utterance was just rage.[1]

---

1   B. B. Warfield, *The Emotional Life of Our Lord* (New York: Ravenio Books, 2013), Kindle.

By 'just rage,' Warfield did not mean *only* rage. Jesus' rage was righteous, intense, and perfectly appropriate. It was *just*. Warfield explains that this 'inwardly restrained fury produced a profound agitation of his whole being, one of the manifestations of which was tears.'

But toward what, and at whom, was this controlled anger directed? Jesus directed His anger at death itself, as well as at the devil whose deception of our original parents led to the sin which brought death into the world. 'Why did the sight of the wailing of Mary and her companions enrage Jesus?' Warfield asks, and then answers his own question: 'The spectacle of the distress of Mary and her companions enraged Jesus because it brought poignantly home to his consciousness the evil of death, its unnaturalness' and caused him to '[burn] with rage against the oppressor of men ... What John does for us in this particular statement is to uncover to us the heart of Jesus, as he wins for us our salvation.' Jesus died in your place so that 'through death He might render powerless him who had the power of death, that is, the devil' (Heb. 2:14-15).

Death is unnatural. It disturbs us, as it should. Therefore, we should not be surprised when we experience the mixture of a wide range of emotions. But, as Christians, godly grief should also deepen our appreciation for the victory which Jesus secured through His own death, burial, and resurrection. Jesus died and rose again to deliver us not only from our sins but also from our fear of death (Heb. 2:14-15).

JESUS KNOWS THE FEELINGS OF ABANDONMENT AND REJECTION

While the Son of God endured the divine wrath against our sin, He cried out, 'My God, my God, why have You forsaken me?' (Ps. 22:1). This anguish was first expressed by King David, but it finds its fullest expression and fulfillment in Jesus, the greater David, whose suffering would atone for our sins once for all. In that moment of time, when the sin debt of humanity was imputed to the sinless one, Jesus experienced abandonment and rejection so that you and I would never have to be turned away by God.

David's cry became Jesus' own cry of abandonment while He hung on the cross (Mark 15:34). Mingled throughout the horrific suffering described here are reassuring truths about the character of God. He is the ultimate source of hope and strength. God is holy, trustworthy, and near to all who trust in Him.

Yet You are holy, You who are enthroned upon the praises of Israel. In You our fathers trusted; they trusted and You rescued them. To You they cried out and they fled to safety; in You they trusted and were not disappointed … Yet You are He who brought me forth from the womb; You made me trust when upon my mother's breasts. I was cast upon You from birth; You have been my God from my mother's womb. (Ps. 22:3-4, 9-10)

Jesus understands the pain that sticks to abandonment and loss. No matter who or what is causing it, there is no sadness, hurt, or loss that Jesus does not know personally.

When Hebrews 4:15 compels us to bring our needs to God's throne of grace, the exhortation is based on the high priestly ministry of Jesus as the One who can 'sympathize with our weaknesses' because He experienced every category of trial and temptation we face. The prophet Isaiah describes the Messiah this way:

He is despised and rejected by men, a Man of sorrows and acquainted with grief. And we hid, as it were, our faces from Him; He was despised, and we did not esteem Him. (Isa. 53:3, NKJV)

Besides feeling abandoned, Jesus endured rejection when He hung on the cross as your sin-bearing Savior. The apostle Peter describes it this way:

(HE) WHO COMMITTED NO sin, NOR WAS ANY DECEIT found IN HIS MOUTH; and while being abusively insulted, He did not insult in return; while suffering, He did not threaten, but kept entrusting Himself to Him who judges righteously. (1 Pet. 2:22-23)

When you feel rejected, or grief tempts you to think no one understands what you're going through, turn your eyes upon Jesus. He understands the agony of your loss and any feelings of abandonment or rejection that may accompany it.

MAIN POINT

Jesus' response to the pain of loss instructs you to consider the goodness of sadness and to entrust your hurts to your faithful heavenly Father.

QUESTIONS FOR REFLECTION

- Jesus cried at His friend's grave. How does thinking about this reality help you in your own times of sorrow? How might it influence the way you respond to the grief expressions of friends and loved ones?

- Jesus' grief was mixed with anger against sin and our enemies: death and the devil. How does knowing that Jesus always expressed righteous anger help you guard your heart from sinful anger? How might holding on to anger, even if it's righteous, harm you or others in times of grief?

- Meditate on Psalm 22. In what ways do you see Jesus as the suffering Savior who can empathize with your sorrow?

8. The Holy Spirit Prays for You

Do you ever feel as if you should pray, but are not sure what to say? This is a common problem when we are grieving. The emotional pain of loss can bring us to a place of not knowing what to say to God. Yet, in the process of our groaning, we can find comfort in knowing how the Holy Spirit plays a unique and unexpected role. Romans 8:26-27 puts it like this:

In the same way the Spirit also helps our weakness; for we do not know how to pray as we should, but the Spirit Himself intercedes for us with groanings too deep for words; and He who searches the hearts knows what the mind of the Spirit is, because He intercedes for the saints according to the will of God.

As creation groans for the fullness of redemption (Rom. 8:22), and just as believers groan while waiting for redemption from their earthly bodies (Rom. 8:23), so the Holy Spirit groans in prayer on our behalf. Three truths concerning the Spirit's ministry of prayer should bring you comfort.

THE SPIRIT PRAYS FOR YOU BECAUSE HE KNOWS YOUR WEAKNESS

The Holy Spirit lives within every believer and helps us in our weakness. Because this is true, He comes to your aid by making your prayers acceptable to God the Father, and He shoulders your burdens. Here, it is important to remind yourself that physical, emotional, and spiritual weaknesses reveal human frailty, yet they are not necessarily the result of sin. As we saw in the last chapter, Jesus, the sinless Son of God, experienced human frailty—enabling Him to now 'sympathize with our weaknesses'—yet He never sinned (Heb. 4:14-15).

As your intercessor, the ascended Christ is acutely aware of your need to be 'strengthened with power through His Spirit in the inner man' (Eph. 3:16). The same Spirit who empowered the Lord Jesus during His time on earth now indwells you and, therefore, He not only knows your weaknesses but is also infinitely able to pray for you accordingly. In this way, the Spirit of Jesus helps your weakness.

THE SPIRIT PRAYS FOR YOU BECAUSE YOU HAVE LIMITED KNOWLEDGE

When one of my daughters was young, she loved to eat pears but couldn't tell when they were ripe. As a result, she would often grab a hard, green pear off the kitchen counter, take one bite, and leave the rest behind. 'It's too hard,' she complained. We often do the same, as Matthew Henry writes, 'We are short-sighted ... like foolish children, that are ready to cry for fruit before it is ripe and fit for them.'[1] We want the fruit that God is preparing for our future. But we want it now, before it is ripe.

In a similar way, when we are grieving, we 'do not know how to pray as we should' (Rom. 8:26). The Spirit prays for us because our knowledge is incomplete. But the Spirit prays according to perfect knowledge. He prays with 'groanings too deep for words.' The Spirit pleads on our behalf with longings which are verbally inexpressible. This is the silent prayer ministry of the Spirit.

---

1   Matthew Henry, *Matthew Henry's Commentary on the Whole Bible*, vol. vi (McLean, VA: MacDonald, 1970), 422.

THE SPIRIT PRAYS FOR US BECAUSE HE ALWAYS KNOWS GOD'S WILL

Paul continues in Romans 8:27, 'He who searches the hearts knows what the mind of the Spirit is.' The omniscient Father always knows what the Spirit is thinking. The Spirit's prayers include groanings that literally cannot be verbalized, but the Father knows and understands the thoughts of the Spirit with no need for words. The Spirit of God knows the thoughts of God (1 Cor. 2:11), and the Father knows the thoughts of the Spirit. The two are always in full agreement.

This is how the Bible came to us—the Spirit translating God's thoughts to us as words (1 Cor. 2:13, 2 Pet. 1:21). Knowing that God reveals His thoughts by the Spirit in the written Word, you may be confident that the non-verbal requests the Spirit prays to the Father on your behalf always perfectly match up with Scripture. The same cannot always be said of your prayers or mine, as R. C. Sproul exhorts:

Professing Christians often ask God to bless or sanction their sin. They are even capable of telling their friends they have prayed about a certain matter and God has given them peace, despite what they prayed for was contrary to his will. Such prayers are thinly veiled acts of blasphemy, and we add insult to God when we dare to announce that his Spirit has sanctioned our sin by giving us peace in our souls. Such a peace is a carnal peace and has nothing to do with the peace that passes understanding, the peace that the Spirit is pleased to grant to those who love God and love his law.[2]

It comes as no surprise that sinful, rebellious people like you and me can generate selfish prayers. We can pray with our mouths, 'Thy will be done,' but mean in our hearts, 'My will be done.' This is where the Spirit helps enormously. The Spirit and the Son make our prayers acceptable to the Father according to His will. We pray, but then, based on those prayers, the Son and the Spirit pray in sync with the will of God.

All three persons in the Trinity are actively involved in caring for you in your time of need. The heavenly Father tunes into your needs. The Son intercedes as your High Priest because He gave His lifeblood to redeem you and become the only gateway to the Father. And when you

---

2   R. C. Sproul, *The Invisible Hand* (Phillipsburg, NJ: P&R, 2003), 209.

do not know how to pray, the Holy Spirit pleads with the Father on your behalf according to His perfect will.

MAIN POINT

The Holy Spirit prays for you when you groan under the weight of the burden of loss.

QUESTIONS FOR REFLECTION

- How should learning about the Holy Spirit's silent prayer ministry affect the way you respond to your suffering?
- In what ways do you see that you are like the short-sighted, foolish children that Matthew Henry describes as being "ready to cry for fruit before it is ripe and fit for them"?
- How does the assurance that the Spirit always prays according to the will of God bring you comfort?

9. Hopelessness and Hope

When I was growing up, I couldn't wait to learn to drive. Finally, in my sophomore year of high school, I was old enough to register for classroom instruction, followed by in-car training. But even though I was in the driver's seat, the instructor seated next to me selected the route and gave the directions. I was holding the steering wheel, but someone else was telling me what to do and where to go. In a similar way, grief can upend our emotions. It can shift our emotions into the driver's seat and relegate our mind, which should be governed by biblical truth, to the passenger's side.

THREE PITFALLS TO AVOID

Grief can leave us emotionally vulnerable. As a result, it's easy to get off course or get stuck in the mud of hopelessness. So, let me caution you to watch out for three common pitfalls in grieving.

Excessive lingering over your loss

When grief lingers too long, it can turn inward and become self-pity. Self-pity, when nursed, can then turn your loss into a little god. I know this from personal experience. Grief becomes excessive when it becomes the reason we cannot trust and obey God in our response. Sadly, I also know this from experience. Therefore, the following words of the Puritan pastor Richard Sibbes help us:

> How will we know when to cease and leave off mourning? The soul has many things to do and it cannot always mourn nor always rejoice. We have mourned enough, when we have overcome our hearts, and brought them to a temper of mourning, and have complained before God, spread the ill of the times before him, and entreated pity from him, having poured out ourselves in prayer. When we have this done, then we have discharged our duty in mourning and must then look upon causes of rejoicing and thanksgiving.[1]

---

1   Richard Sibbes and David B. MacKinnon, ed. *Refreshment for the Soul* (Edinburgh: Banner of Truth Trust, 2022), 27.

Just as King David got stuck after the death of his son and had to be exhorted to get back to work, so we sometimes need help to get unstuck (2 Sam. 19:1-7). If you suspect you are stuck in your grief, begin thinking of reasons to rejoice and express thanks to the Lord. Enlist the help of a spiritual friend or mentor if you need help to bring God's many blessings to remembrance.

Anger at God

In an earlier chapter, we noticed the mixture of grief and anger in Jesus' response to the death of his friend. Jesus was angry at death and the devil, but His anger was always righteous. In contrast, our anger—even if it begins righteous—easily slides toward sinful responses to life's hurts. Worst of all, our anger can sometimes slide toward God.

Since anger is essentially a judgment that something is wrong, Jim Newheiser explains:

It is never permissible ... to be angry with God. Such anger presumes that God has somehow been unjust. Furthermore, the person who is angry with God places himself above God as His judge, which is both wrong and dangerous.[2]

When you feel the pain of loss, you form a judgment about it. That judgment and its emotional response make up the components of anger, frustration, and irritability. However, anger at God only makes matters worse; it separates you from One who cares the most about your grief and has the power to heal your heart.

This does not mean you cannot cry out to God in honest laments of deep pain, even complaining to Him about injustice. In fact, God invites you to do just that. But biblical lament complains *to* God, not *about* God. Mark Vroegop defines lament as 'a prayer in pain that leads to trust ... It is the path from heartbreak to hope.'[3] Biblical lament follows a four-step process: (1) turn to God, (2) complain to God, (3) ask God for help, and (4) choose to trust. As you bring your hurts to the Lord, you can also counsel yourself, as David does, with biblical wisdom: 'Cease from anger and forsake

---

2   Jim Newheiser, *Help! My Anger Is Out of Control* (Wapwallopen, PA: Shepherd Press, 2015), 47-48.

3   Mark Vroegop, *Dark Clouds, Deep Mercy* (Wheaton, IL: Crossway Books, 2019), 28.

wrath; do not fret; it leads only to evildoing'
(Ps. 37:8).

Isolation

God never intended for you to suffer alone.
One of the clearest pieces of evidence of this
is the brilliant design of the local church.
Romans 12:15-16 exhorts believers this way:

> *Rejoice with those who rejoice, and weep with
> those who weep. Be of the same mind toward
> one another; do not be haughty in mind, but
> associate with the lowly. Do not be wise in
> your own estimation.*

For Christians, this is the way it is: rejoicing and
weeping mingle together on life's journey.
But this is not a journey that God wants you
to walk alone. Therefore, cultivating humility
is essential.

One way you humbly walk through dark
valleys is by participating in the weekly
worship gathering on Sundays. God-centered
singing of 'psalms and hymns and spiritual
songs' with other believers will nurture a heart
of thankfulness and praise and keep the eyes
of your heart looking at Christ (Col. 3:16).
However, sometimes, your emotions may not

want to cooperate, and you may not *feel* like singing. In that case, listening to others sing can infuse strength into your inner person as it gently applies its healing truth. Also, congregational prayer allows you to piggyback on the sturdy faith of other believers, which carries you to the throne of grace where you receive divine help in your time of need.

Therefore, the best decision you can make is to return to worship with your local church family as soon as possible. Let God's people come alongside you and care for you, even if they do it imperfectly. Avoid the pitfall of isolation. You are not alone.

HOPE-FILLED GRIEVING

All people grieve, but those who know Jesus grieve differently. We grieve with hope—the hope of heaven. The apostle Paul informs us of this difference between believers and unbelievers:

But we do not want you to be uninformed, brethren, about those who are asleep, so that you will not grieve as do the rest who have no hope. For if we believe that Jesus died and rose again, even so God will bring with Him those who have fallen asleep in Jesus. (1 Thess. 4:13-14)

As believers in the resurrected, ascended, and soon-returning King, we can grieve with hope because we are certain about our long-term future. After Jesus returns, He will 'wipe away every tear from [our] eyes; and there will no longer be any death; there will no longer be any mourning, or crying, or pain; the first things have passed away. And He who sits on the throne [says], "Behold, I am making all things new"' (Rev. 21:4-5). For this reason, Paul counsels us to 'not grieve as do the rest who have no hope.' The basis of his admonishment is the return of the Lord to complete the redemption of His people.

In the presence of the Savior and Judge we will never grieve again. Therefore, Tim Challies comforts us with these words:

> The Christian faith offers the promise of a future in which this earth will be renewed and restored, in which all pain and sorrow will be comforted, in which all evil and sin will be removed.[4]

If you are in Christ then death, grief, and loss can never hurt you again. Sin and the devil will be no more. The resurrection once and for

---

4   Challies *Seasons of Sorrow*, 5.

all removes the sting of death (1 Cor. 15:55). Instead of grieving like those who have no hope, we can look forward to hearing our Savior say, 'enter into the joy of your master' (Matt. 25:23).

MAIN POINT

Grief makes you vulnerable to other powerful emotions taking over the steering wheel and, therefore, you need to renew your mind with truth, and lean on the Lord to strengthen your will.

QUESTIONS FOR REFLECTION

- Which of the three pitfalls addressed in this chapter do you find yourself most vulnerable to?
- Whom in your church family can you reach out to if you get overwhelmed by sorrow?
- Read Revelation 21:1-5. How might meditating on these verses help you? How do they inform your prayers?

10. Be an Avenue, not a Cul-de-sac

The rural subdivision that I grew up in had three cul-de-sacs, but we knew them as circular *dead ends*. My brothers and friends and I loved to ride our bikes from one cul-de-sac to another—around and around all day long. Grief can become like that if we're not careful. When we don't view loss through a biblical lens or we fail to respond to our suffering with childlike trust in our good Father, we may find ourselves going around in circles or getting stuck at a dead end.

In this chapter, I want to help you to understand and appreciate some of the purposes that God has for your suffering, as well as comprehend how the Holy Spirit can use grief and loss to shape you into a more sensitive comforter of others.

YOU ARE A COMFORTER-IN-TRAINING

Instead of being a cul-de-sac, you are an avenue—a pathway for God's comfort to spread to others. This principle is the primary emphasis of 2 Corinthians 1:3-5:

Blessed be the God and Father of our Lord Jesus Christ, the Father of mercies and God of all comfort, who comforts us in all our affliction so that we will be able to comfort those who are in any affliction with the comfort with which we ourselves are comforted by God. For just as the sufferings of Christ are ours in abundance, so also our comfort is abundant through Christ.

In this passage, we see four truths that will encourage your spiritual growth during and after your time of suffering. First, God is the 'Father of mercies and God of all comfort.' God sees you in your present suffering through His eyes of mercy and is ready to dispense comfort at any moment you need it. Indeed, He 'comforts [you] in all [your] affliction.' Second, suffering expands the reach of your ministry. One reason God comforts believers in our affliction is 'so that we will be able to comfort' others who are experiencing similar trials. Right now, in your time of sorrow, God is preparing you for future opportunities to bless and help others. Third, suffering authenticates your ministry by making your delivery of Christ-centered comfort more real—more believable—to others who hurt. Fourth, both suffering and comfort are yours 'in abundance' through Christ. Just as Job asked his grieving wife, so we must learn to say with contentment, 'Shall we indeed accept good from God and not accept adversity?' (Job 2:10). Surely we must accept both! The more we are being conformed to the image of Christ, the more we will be able to accept both blessing and trial with gratitude and faith.

REMEMBER GOD'S PURPOSE FOR YOUR SUFFERING

A common Scripture we turn to in times of loss is Romans 8:28–29, and for good reason. It says:

And we know that God causes all things to work together for good to those who love God, to those who are called according to His purpose. For those whom He foreknew, He also predestined to become conformed to the image of His Son.

Though you should avoid carelessly quoting these verses to someone else in the immediate throws of their loss, they contain

79

three rich, comforting truths to apply to your heart. First, *all things*—even bad things— are employed by God to accomplish good in the lives of believers. Therefore, if you are a believer in Jesus Christ, then you can know without a doubt that God is working out His good purpose in your life right at this moment—even if you cannot see it. Second, *it is God who causes* all things to work toward your good. This is not a trite 'things will work out in the end' or 'whatever will be will be' kind of fatalism. But God is actively working to develop your faith through this trial. Third, *the ultimate good* which God is working all things in your life toward is that of shaping you into the image of Christ. The best *good* for you is that you become more like Jesus. Therefore, one of the most helpful questions you can learn to ask is, *Lord, how can I become more like You because of this trial and pain?*

START BY JUST BEING THERE

In December 2009, my mom died of a massive brain bleed. She left us so quickly that I couldn't get to the hospital in time to say goodbye. Afterward, many people surrounded our family with love and care, but one thing I remember more than others is the faces of the people who attended the pre-service funeral visitation. Former neighbors and childhood friends who I hadn't seen for decades greeted me, shook my hand, or hugged me. They told me how sorry they were for my loss and expressed kind words about Mom. Many even took off work to attend. I will never forget them *just being there*. When it comes to comforting others who are grieving loss, we often think we must know exactly what to say. However, most of the time, we don't need to say much more than 'I'm sorry.' Most importantly, we just need to be there.

The friends of the Old Testament patriarch Job forgot this too quickly and, therefore, will forever be known as 'miserable comforters' (Job 16:2). They earned this label because when they opened their mouths, their verbal counsel comprised one basic message: 'Job, your losses are your fault.' However, let's not miss the one thing they did right. In the immediate wake of losing his ten children to death, and his possessions to destruction, Job's friends did one thing right. They were there for him.

When they lifted up their eyes at a distance and did not recognize him, they raised their voices and wept. And each of them tore his robe and they threw dust over their heads toward the sky. Then they sat down on the ground with him for seven days and seven nights with no one speaking a word to him, for they saw that his pain was very great. (Job 2:12-13)

The quiet presence of his friends contributed to Job's immediate need for tender comfort. They simply showed up. And you can do the same.

When someone you love loses someone they love, it is usually most helpful if you carefully guard your mouth, open your ears, and, if appropriate, offer a tender touch. Take time to weep with those who weep (Rom. 12:15). Don't be too quick to offer answers (especially in the case of a suicide). Let them cry. Give them freedom to feel nothing, to simply be numb from the shock of it all. Let them know you care by simply being there. Perhaps pray briefly with them. And silently pray for yourself to speak wisely when the time is right.

Quiet presence is an important part of your ministry to others in times of loss; however, it is not sufficient for the long haul. When it is appropriate, you need to learn to gently speak words of grace and truth for their comfort and the nurturing of their faith in Christ (Eph. 4:15). Saturate your words with God's words but avoid a preachy manner or tone. Pursue gentleness (1 Tim. 6:11). There may come a time later down the road for a firmer exhortation, if they allow their grief to become self-consuming, and you observe them going in circles or getting stuck at a dead end. However, even then, be careful that you speak for their benefit, not simply to make yourself feel better for getting something off your chest. Come alongside them with God's promise of comfort (2 Cor. 1:3-4) and compassion (Col. 3:12) in a timely manner (Eph. 4:29). Aim to practice incarnational ministry, that is, strive to be like Jesus, who is "full of [both] grace and truth" (John 1:14).

Healthy grieving continues when you view the comfort you receive from God as an avenue, not a cul-de-sac. It's a through-street, not a dead end. Your need for comfort is very important. Please don't misunderstand me! But it is not the end-all. You are a comforter-in-training who is growing in your appreciation of the good purposes of God for suffering. Don't think you need to be a professional people-helper to be used by the Spirit to comfort others. What your family member or friend needs most from you is to just be there.

MAIN POINT

God comforts you in your sorrow not only for your benefit but to be a conduit of mercy and grace to others in their time of need.

QUESTIONS FOR REFLECTION

- In your grief, are you ever tempted to think it is all about you? How can you pray for the Lord to help you grow in compassion toward others?
- In what ways do you see the Lord using your suffering to make you more like Jesus?
- Who in your life is currently grieving? This week, how could you show them that you care and are there for them?

Appendix A: What do I do now?

- When life hurts, we all have our favorite escape routes and hiding places where we go to avoid additional pain. Therefore, begin to form a personal 'theology of refuge.' Begin by meditating on Psalms 23, 46, 90, and 121 and journaling the truths you learn about God, what He is like, why He is your best hiding place, etc. As time goes on, consider adding other Scripture passages to your theology of refuge.

- Memorize a few key 'comfort food' Scriptures to feed your soul. These can help turn your mind and heart toward the Lord on hard days. Choose from: Psalm 34:18; 46:1; 56:8; 91:4; 121:1; Lamentations 3:22-23; Isaiah 43:2; Romans 8:18, 38-39;

2 Corinthians 1:3-4; Hebrews 4:15; James 1:2-5; 1 Peter 1:3-5.

- Using one of the above Scriptures, write and mail a kind note of comfort to someone you know who is grieving loss of some kind. Include thoughts from the selected Scripture and assure them you are praying for them. After a week, call or text with a suggested day and time to pick them up for lunch or grab some coffee. Go with a listening heart.

- Anxiety often escalates during times of grief—there are so many *what ifs*. In a journal or notebook, write everything you are currently anxious about. Then turn this care list into a prayer list: take each care to the Lord.

- In times of loss, the Lord wants us to talk to Him about what hurts. Read Psalm 13 and then use it as a prayer guide.

- Consider re-reading this book with a friend, one chapter at a time (perhaps out loud). Discuss the reflection questions and pray for each other.

Appendix B: Other Books on this Topic

BOOKS ON GRIEF & LOSS

Challies, Tim. *Seasons of Sorrow* (Zondervan, 2022).

Guthrie, Nancy. *What Grieving People Wish You Knew about What Really Helps (and What Really Hurts)* (Crossway, 2016).

Tautges, Paul. *A Small Book for the Hurting Heart* (New Growth Press, 2020).

Welch, Edward. *Someone I Know Is Grieving* (New Growth Press, 2023).

BOOKS AND MINIBOOKS ON ANXIETY

De Courcy, Philip. *Help! I'm Anxious* (Shepherd Press, 2018).

Moll, Lucy Ann. *Help! I Get Panic Attacks* (Shepherd Press, 2019).

Tautges, Paul. *Anxiety: Knowing God's Peace* (P&R Publishing, 2019).

Welch, Edward T. *A Student's Guide to Anxiety* (Christian Focus Publications, 2020).

BOOKS AND MINIBOOKS ON ANGER AND BITTERNESS

Newheiser, Jim. *Help! My Anger Is Out of Control* (Shepherd Press, 2015).

Tautges, Paul. *Bitterness: When You Can't Move On* (New Growth Press, 2022).

Viars, Stephen. *Overcoming Bitterness* (Baker Books, 2021).

BOOKS AND MINIBOOKS ON DEPRESSION

Eswine, Zack. *Spurgeon's Sorrows: Realistic Hope for Those who Suffer from Depression* (Christian Focus Publications, 2015).

Hodges, Charles. *Good Mood, Bad Mood: Help and Hope for Depression and Bipolar Disorder* (Shepherd Press, 2013).

Kwasny, John. *A Student's Guide to Depression* (Christian Focus Publications, 2022).

Trahan, Carol. *Help! I'm Depressed* (Shepherd Press, 2014).

Welch, Ed. *Hope for the Depressed* (New Growth Press, 2010).

BOOKS AND MINIBOOKS ON SUICIDE

Powlison, David. *Grieving a Suicide* (New Growth Press, 2010).

Ray, Bruce. *Help! My Friend Is Suicidal* (Shepherd Press, 2014).

Ray, Bruce. *Help! Someone I Love Died by Suicide* (Shepherd Press, 2019).

BOOKS ON GROWING IN CHRIST

Bridges, Jerry. *Transforming Grace*. New ed. (NavPress, 2017).

Tautges, Paul. *Remade: Embracing Your Complete Identity in Christ* (P&R Publishing, 2023).

Appendix C: Bible Chapters that Bring Comfort

The Security and Care of God
When you feel weak, threatened, or need strength, read Psalm 46.
When fear threatens to overshadow your peace, read Psalm 23.
When discouragement casts a dark cloud over you, read Isaiah 40.
When you doubt God's love, read Romans 8.
When you wonder if God is good, read Psalm 111.

Help for Your Emotions
When you are anxious, read Matthew 6.
When you sense bitterness settling into your heart, read Genesis 50.
When the challenges of life seem bigger than God, read Psalm 90.
When God seems far away, read Psalm 139.

When you need peace of mind and rest for
your soul, read Matthew 11.
When you want to think more deeply about
happiness, read Matthew 5.

Questions about Jesus
Who is Jesus Christ? Read John 20; 1 John 5.
Why did Jesus come to earth? Read Isaiah 53;
Romans 5.
Why does the Bible call Jesus the mediator?
Read 1 Timothy 2.
How does God save sinners? Read
Ephesians 2.

The Promise of Eternal Life
When you feel guilty, read Psalm 103.
When you need forgiveness, pray
through Psalm 51.
When you are wondering about eternal life,
read John 3; 1 John 5
When you wonder what faith looks like,
read Hebrews 11.
When you want to think about heaven,
read Revelation 21.

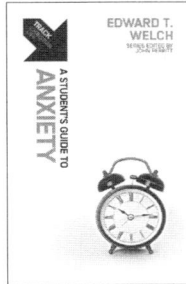

Track: Anxiety
A Student's Guide to Anxiety
Edward T. Welch

- How to deal with anxiety
- For younger adults
- Part of the 'Track' series

We all know the feeling. That nervous, jittery, tense feeling that tells you that something bad is just ahead. Anxiety can be overwhelming. But the Bible has plenty to say to people who are anxious. This book will help us to take our eyes off our circumstances and fix them on God.

Edward T. Welch
Counselor & Faculty at Christian Counseling and Educational Foundation and author of 'When People Are Big and God is Small', 'Running Scared', and 'Shame Interrupted'

ISBN: 978-1-5271-0450-1

Reformed Youth Ministries (RYM) exists to serve the Church in reaching and equipping youth for Christ. Passing on the faith to the next generation has been RYM's mission since it began. In 1972, three youth workers who shared a passion for biblical teaching to high school students surveyed the landscape of youth ministry conferences. What they found was a primary emphasis on fun and games, not God's Word. They launched a conference that focused on the preaching and teaching of God's Word – RYM. Over the last five decades RYM has grown from a single summer conference into three areas of ministry: conferences, training, and resources.

- **Conferences:** RYM hosts multiple summer conferences for local church groups in a variety of locations across the United States. Conferences are for either middle school or high school students and their leaders.
- **Training:** RYM launched an annual Youth Leader Training (YLT) event in 2008. YLT is

for anyone serving with youth in the local church. YLT has grown steadily through the years and is now offered in multiple locations. RYM also offers a Church Internship Program in partnering local churches, youth leader coaching and youth ministry consulting services.

- **Resources:** RYM offers a growing array of resources for leaders, parents, and students. Several Bible studies are available as free downloads (new titles regularly added). RYM hosts multiple podcasts available on numerous platforms: The Local Youth Worker, Parenting Today, and The RYM Student Podcast. To access free downloads, for podcast information, and access to many additional ministry tools visit us on the web – rym.org.

RYM is a 501(c)(3) non-profit organization. Our mission is made possible through the generous support of individuals, churches, foundations and businesses that share our mission to serve the Church in reaching and equipping youth for Christ. If you would like to partner with RYM in reaching and equipping the next generation for Christ please visit rym.org/donate.

Christian Focus Publications

Our mission statement —

STAYING FAITHFUL

In dependence upon God we seek to impact the world through literature faithful to His infallible Word, the Bible. Our aim is to ensure that the Lord Jesus Christ is presented as the only hope to obtain forgiveness of sin, live a useful life and look forward to heaven with Him.

Our books are published in four imprints:

CHRISTIAN
FOCUS

Popular works including biographies, commentaries, basic doctrine and Christian living.

CHRISTIAN
HERITAGE

Books representing some of the best material from the rich heritage of the church.

MENTOR

Books written at a level suitable for Bible College and seminary students, pastors, and other serious readers. The imprint includes commentaries, doctrinal studies, examination of current issues and church history.

CF4•K

Children's books for quality Bible teaching and for all age groups: Sunday school curriculum, puzzle and activity books; personal and family devotional titles, biographies and inspirational stories — because you are never too young to know Jesus!

Christian Focus Publications Ltd,
Geanies House, Fearn, Ross-shire,
IV20 1TW, Scotland, United Kingdom.
www.christianfocus.com
blog.christianfocus.com